PET GUINEA PIG

by Robin Nelson

Lerner Publications Company · Minneapolis

A guinea pig is an **animal.**

Guinea pigs make
good **pets.**

Guinea pigs can look
very different.

Guinea pigs can be many
different colors.

Guinea pigs need
a clean **cage.**

Guinea pigs need to be
warm and dry.

Guinea pigs love to eat.

Guinea pigs need food
every day.

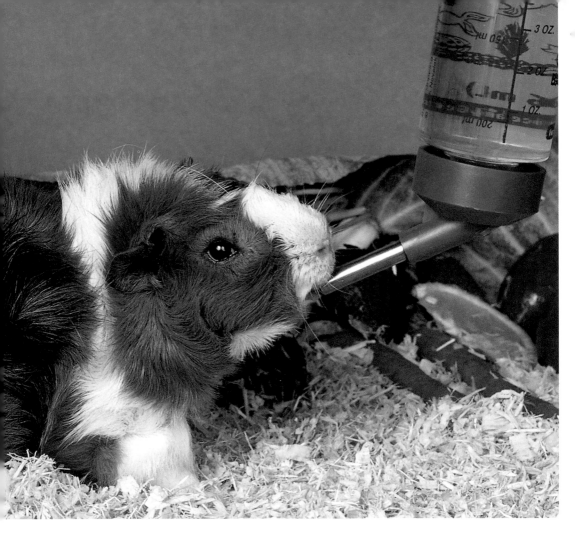

Guinea pigs need fresh
water every day.

Guinea pigs need to
chew on wood.

Guinea pigs need **exercise.**

Guinea pigs like to **explore.**

Guinea pigs need company.

Guinea pigs like to be held.

We like to watch
our guinea pig.

We like taking care of guinea pigs.

There are many different kinds of guinea pigs.

Smooth-haired guinea pigs are popular as pets.

Each hair on a smooth-haired agouti has a mix of two colors.

A crested guinea pig has smooth hair all over its body except on its head.

Long-haired Peruvians are often seen in pet shows.

An Abyssinian has whirls of hair called rosettes all over its body.

Fun Guinea Pig Facts

 Guinea pigs are not pigs.

 Guinea pigs do not have tails.

 Guinea pigs live to be 5 to 8 years old.

 Guinea pigs are very "talkative." They make many different kinds of noises to communicate with other guinea pigs and humans.

Some guinea pigs like quiet music. It helps them to relax.

 Guinea pigs have excellent hearing.

 A guinea pig's teeth continue to grow all of its life. Guinea pigs keep their teeth the right length by chewing on wood and other hard objects.

Glossary

 animal – anything alive that is not a plant

 cage – a type of box where small animals are kept

 exercise – moving your body around

 explore – to go into a place you have never been before to see what is there

 pets – animals that live with people

Index

The photographs in this book are reproduced through the courtesy of: © Carolyn A. McKeone/Photo Researchers Inc., cover, pp. 4 (top left and bottom left), 6, 18 (bottom), 19 (bottom), 22 (second from top); © Norvia Behling, pp. 2, 8, 9, 10, 12, 14, 18 (top), 22 (top and middle); PhotoDisc Royalty Free, pp. 3, 22 (bottom); © Charles R. Belinky/Photo Researchers Inc., p. 4 (top right); © Kathy Merrifield/Photo Researchers Inc., pp. 4 (bottom right), 13, 19 (middle), 22 (second from bottom); © H. Reinhard/OKAPIA/Photo Researchers Inc., p. 5; © Joan Balzarini, pp. 7, 19 (top); © Christine Steimer/OKAPIA/Photo Researchers Inc., p. 11; © Petit Format/Photo Researchers, Inc., p. 15; © Jeff Isaac Greenberg/Photo Researchers Inc., p. 16; © Laura Dwight/CORBIS, p. 17.

Lerner Publications Company
A division of Lerner Publishing Group
241 First Avenue North
Minneapolis, MN 55401 USA

Website address: www.lernerbooks.com

Library of Congress Cataloging-in-Publication Data

Nelson, Robin, 1971–
    Pet guinea pig / by Robin Nelson.
        p.   cm. — (First step nonfiction)
    Summary: An introduction to pet guinea pigs and their basic needs.
    ISBN: 0–8225–1268–8 (lib. bdg. : alk. paper)
    1. Guinea pigs as pets—Juvenile literature. [1. Guinea pigs. 2. Pets.]
    I. Title. II. Series.
    SF459.G9 N45 2003
    636.9'3592—dc21   2001005974

Manufactured in the United States of America
2 3 4 5 6 7 – DP – 09 08 07 06 05 04